JUST say YES!

DEVOTIONAL

Other Abingdon Press Resources by Robert Schnase

Five Practices of Fruitful Living

Five Practices of Fruitful Congregations

Seven Levers: Missional Strategies for Conferences

Just Say Yes! Unleashing People for Ministry

Just Say Yes! Leader Guide

Just Say Yes! Participant Guide

Just Say Yes! DVD

Author of *Five Practices of Fruitful Congregations*

Robert Schnase

with Angela Olsen

JUST *say* YES!

UNLEASHING PEOPLE FOR MINISTRY

DEVOTIONAL

Abingdon Press

Nashville

JUST SAY YES! DEVOTIONAL:
UNLEASHING PEOPLE FOR MINISTRY

This book is printed on acid-free paper.

ISBN: 978-1-5018-2579-8

References in parenthesis indicate page numbers in *Just Say Yes! Unleashing People for Ministry* by Robert Schnase (Nashville: Abingdon Press, 2015).

16 17 18 19 20 21 22 23 24 25—10 9 8 7 6 5 4 3 2 1
MANUFACTURED IN THE UNITED STATES OF AMERICA

Contents

Introduction

Thank you for joining us for a month of intentionally saying *Yes* to God's work in your life. This sermon series and devotional is based on the book *Just Say Yes! Unleashing People for Ministry* by Robert Schnase. The core principle of the book is that "growing churches say *Yes* to ministries that declining churches say *No* to. They have figured out how to foster creativity, nurture the call of God among their people, value innovation, and take initiative. They have learned to adapt and learn and respond and grow" (11).

This type of growth means more and more people becoming followers of Jesus Christ—more and more disciples growing in the love of God and neighbor, more and more people working to transform the world in Jesus's name.

Passionate people, like you, are feeling the call of God in their lives and dreaming about how to make the world a better place. Yet too often, these creative people are discouraged or shut down before they can even begin. This book and devotional challenges us to respond to Christ-centered new ideas and opportunities with positivity, not fear and negativity. At the heart of this devotional is this call: "Don't operate with *No* as your default response to all things new. Give the Spirit room to move. Be the person God works through rather than the person God has to work around. Leave a legacy of encouragement, of support, of prayerful discernment. Unleash people for ministry" (13).

This experience is designed to empower you to unleash yourself and others in response to God's invitation.

In *Just Say Yes!* Robert Schnase offers some missional assumptions to help us counteract our human tendency toward responding *No* to new ideas and challenges. These missional assumptions help us say *Yes* to using our gifts, talents, and passions for Jesus Christ. Therefore, the devotions each week will focus on a missional assumption to keep us centered on Christ and connected to the power of the Holy Spirit.

Week 1: Just Say Yes *to the Holy Spirit*

This week we will delve into the profound and transformative experience of saying *Yes* to Jesus Christ through the power of the Holy Spirit. Through this intimate connection, the Holy Spirit gives each person gifts. These gifts are crucial to the work of Christ in the world. So this week's missional assumption is "everyone has gifts for ministry" (55).

Week 2: Just Say Yes *to Your Calling*

Building on week 1, this week's missional assumption is "God calls everyone to service and ministry" (57). Our focus will be discerning where your gifts, talents, and passions meet the deep needs of the world. In that intersection, you will find your calling.

Week 3: Just Say Yes *to Growth*

Saying *Yes* to Jesus Christ requires us to grow in knowledge of ourselves and who God created us to be. In order to do this, we must continually and intentionally live as disciples. Our missional assumption this week is "the ministries of the church should foster spiritual growth and discipleship" (59).

Week 4: Just Say Yes *to Encouragement*

Our missional assumption is "the work of the church is to encourage people in their callings"(62). Schnase calls this a "permission-giving" culture. Each church member can be part of building this type of church. "The most direct and personal way to contribute to a permission-giving environment is through offering the ministry of encouragement" (112).

Each weekly devotion offers a scripture focus, insights from the *Just Say Yes!* book, questions to ponder, a prayer, and a weekly challenge. These devotions will take approximately thirty to forty-five minutes to complete. You can go through them in one sitting or over several days. You are encouraged to dig deeper into creating a permission-giving church culture by reading the book *Just Say Yes! Unleashing People for Ministry*. After you complete this devotional, may you continue to just say *Yes* to Jesus Christ as you are unleashed for ministry.

Week 1

Just Say *Yes* to the Holy Spirit

Scripture Focus

Brothers and sisters, I don't want you to be ignorant about spiritual gifts. You know that when you were Gentiles you were often misled by false gods that can't even speak. So I want to make it clear to you that no one says, "Jesus is cursed!" when speaking by God's Spirit, and no one can say, "Jesus is Lord," except by the Holy Spirit. There are different spiritual gifts but the same Spirit; and there are different ministries and the same Lord; and there are different activities but the same God who produces all of them in everyone. A demonstration of the Spirit is given to each person for the common good. A word of wisdom is given by the Spirit to one person, a word of knowledge to another according to the same Spirit, faith to still another by the same Spirit, gifts of healing to another in the one Spirit, performance of miracles to another, prophecy to another, the ability to tell spirits apart to another, different kinds of tongues to another, and the interpretation of the tongues to another. All these things are produced by the one and same Spirit who gives what he wants to each person.

Christ is just like the human body—a body is a unit and has many parts; and all the parts of the body are one body, even though there are many. (1 Cor 12:1-12)

Insights from *Just Say Yes!*

Missional Assumption: Everyone Has Gifts for Ministry

"From the earliest scriptures, Christian leaders have discerned that everyone who belongs to Christ and seeks to follow Christ is gifted by the Holy Spirit to contribute to the ministry of Christ. Just as everyone is part of the body of Christ with distinct functions to perform as the parts of a body—eye, mouth, ears—each serving a different purpose, so also everyone has spiritual gifts that the mission of Christ needs for strengthening the church and its witness. . . .

All who belong to Christ are encouraged to discover their gifts and to cultivate them for building up the church. Christ expects us to use our gifts." (55–56)

Questions to Ponder

- When was a time you experienced the power and presence of the Holy Spirit? Did you know Jesus said *Yes* to you first and gave you power through the Holy Spirit to respond with a *Yes* (1 Cor 12:3)?

- Schnase offers a list of gifts highlighted in the New Testament: "administration, apostleship, compassion, discernment, encouragement, evangelism, exhortation, faith, giving, healing, helping, tongues, interpretation of tongues, knowledge, leadership, miracles, prophecy, servanthood, shepherding, teaching, and wisdom" (56). If you have taken a spiritual gift inventory, which gifts do you have and how are you using them now? If you have not taken an inventory, which gifts do you think God has given you? Is it hard for you to believe the gifts God has given you are crucial for the work of Christ?

- What does it mean to you when you read 1 Corinthians 12:7: "A demonstration of the Spirit is given to each person for the common good"?

Prayer

Empowering spirit, please help me to continually call Jesus Lord of my life. Help me to understand and embrace the gifts you have given me. Strengthen me to fulfill my role in your work here on earth. In the name of Jesus Christ, amen.

Weekly Challenge

Take some time this week to explore what gifts God has given you. Even if you have already completed a spiritual gifts inventory in the past do an assessment again this week. An online option can be found at http://www.umc.org/what-we-believe/spiritual-gifts-online-assessment, or you can ask the staff at church for options. After you receive your results, take some time in self-reflection and prayer to explore how to use these gifts faithfully.

Week 2

Just Say *Yes* to Your Calling

Scripture Focus

Then Jesus said to his disciples, "All who want to come after me must say no to themselves, take up their cross, and follow me. All who want to save their lives will lose them. But all who lose their lives because of me will find them." (Matt 16:24-25)

Whoever wants to be first among you will be your slave—just as the Human One didn't come to be served but rather to serve and to give his life to liberate many people." (Matt 20:27-28)

Insights from *Just Say Yes!*

Missional Assumption: God Calls Everyone to Service and Ministry

"God's call causes us to go places we might not choose to go if left to our own preferences. It's not that we literally hear a Hollywood-like voice from God booming out loud in clearly resonant tones. Rather, our relationship with Christ, our prayer life, our participation in worship, or our study of scripture stimulates an inner urge or strong impulse. God awakens us to a particular sense of responsibility to act. We become aware of an unmet need even as we become aware of particular gifts, passions, and experiences we ourselves can offer to address the need on behalf of Christ. . . .

The real you, your true self, is discovered in letting Christ lead you into serving others with compassion." (57–58, 59)

Questions to Ponder

- What does it mean to say *No* to yourself and *Yes* to following Jesus Christ? Is letting go of selfish tendencies and focusing on others a scary or freeing idea for your life?

- Do you feel a call from God on your life or have you understood a "calling" as only for clergy? How does it impact your life to know every follower of Jesus Christ has a "calling"?

____

____

____

- There are thousands of self-help books on the market, but scripture and *Just Say Yes!* say finding your true self happens in serving others. Does this resonate with your experience or challenge your understanding of the real you? When you served others what went through your mind and how did you feel?

____

____

____

Prayer

Compassionate God, help me clearly hear your call on my life. Awaken in me an understanding of how to use my gifts, talents, and passions faithfully. Help me find my true self through serving others. In the name of Jesus Christ, amen.

Weekly Challenge

As described in *Just Say Yes!*, create a graph (see example on the next page) with your gifts, talents, and passions on the bottom, and then write down unmet needs or places of suffering in the world that tug at your heart on the left side (58). The place where these two sides intersect is an excellent place to start answering your God-given calling. Have you heard of a ministry or organization that might be working to meet the needs you listed and could use your gifts? If so, contact them to inquire about helping. If not, start prayerfully considering championing an effort related to your calling.

Needs I See in the World That Break My Heart			
Illiteracy in Children	I could offer my skills to write about the needs. Possibly educate people at church and beyond.	I could donate books to after school Christian reading/tutoring ministries.	I could volunteer to read with kids at an after school reading ministry.
Kids in Foster Care	I could offer my skills to write about the needs. Possibly educate people at church and beyond.	I could donate items to ministries that help kids in transition.	I could train to do respite care for foster care families.
	Writing	Generosity	Good with Children
	My Passion, Gifts, and Talents		

Week 3

Just Say *Yes* to Growth

Scripture Focus

He gave some apostles, some prophets, some evangelists, and some pastors and teachers. His purpose was to equip God's people for the work of serving and building up the body of Christ until we all reach the unity of faith and knowledge of God's Son. God's goal is for us to become mature adults—to be fully grown, measured by the standard of the fullness of Christ. As a result, we aren't supposed to be infants any longer who can be tossed and blown around by every wind that comes from teaching with deceitful scheming and the tricks people play to deliberately mislead others. Instead, by speaking the truth with love, let's grow in every way into Christ, who is the head. The whole body grows from him, as it is joined and held together by all the supporting ligaments. The body makes itself grow in that it builds itself up with love as each one does its part. (Eph 4:11-16)

Insights from *Just Say Yes!*

Missional Assumption: The Ministries of the Church Should Foster Spiritual Growth and Discipleship

"*Disciple* is derived from *discipulus* and *discere*, words that mean *learner* and *follower*. A disciple of Jesus Christ is someone who desires to follow Christ, who believes his teachings and tries to act accordingly" (59). The goal is to move people on the path of sanctification, increasing in love of God and neighbor. "These disciples are not crippled by obvious sinful patterns, are devoted in personal prayer life and community worship, are attentive to the needs and injustices of the world and offer themselves generously to help, are attentive to God and demonstrate significant growth in the fruit of the spirit—gentleness, kindness, patience." (60)

Questions to Ponder

- In order to faithfully use your gifts, you must stay intimately connected with God. What ways are you practicing being a disciple of Jesus Christ, a learner, and follower? Are you consistently participating in the means of grace that help disciples grow: praying, worshipping, participating in the sacraments, participating in small group Bible study, and serving others?

- What are characteristics of a mature disciple? Can you name some areas of maturity in your life and other areas you want God to strengthen this year?

- This week's scripture focus illustrates being joined together and held by supporting ligaments (Eph 4:16). How are you staying connected to Jesus Christ through the supporting ministries of the church? Are you experiencing the upbuilding of love and accountability to grow in love? If so, how can you invite more people into that experience? If not, are there ways you can intentionally choose to connect with other Christ followers?

Prayer

God of growth, thank you for the gifts you have given me for the common good. Allow me to see areas of my life where I need to grow and mature in order to fully use those gifts. Help me stay intimately connected to your body so I can continually grow in "love, joy, peace, patience, kindness, goodness, faithfulness, gentleness, and self-control" (Gal 5:22-23). In the name of Jesus Christ, amen.

Weekly Challenge

Through these weeks of devotion, you are developing an understanding of your gifts, your passion, and your calling. A crucial piece of growing as a disciple is being in covenant with other believers. These groups can offer encouragement, build you up in love, and challenge you to keep your motives Christ-centered. If you are already in a group, explore some possible studies to help develop your calling to serve others. If you are not currently in a group, prayerfully seek out an opportunity. Please ask your church staff for short-term studies, ministry events, and other learning opportunities that will help strengthen your ability to use your spiritual gifts and answer your call to ministry.

These excellent group studies are available at Cokesbury.com or your favorite bookseller:

Just Say Yes! Study by Robert Schnase with Angela Olsen (Nashville: Abingdon Press, 2016).

Five Marks of a Methodist Study by Magrey DeVega and Steve Harper (Nashville: Abingdon Press, 2016).

Covenant Bible Study (Nashville: Abingdon Press, 2014).

Week 4

Just Say *Yes* to Encouragement

Scripture Focus

And let us consider each other carefully for the purpose of sparking love and good deeds. Don't stop meeting together with other believers, which some people have gotten into the habit of doing. Instead, encourage each other, especially as you see the day drawing near. (Heb 10:24-25)

I really want to see you to pass along some spiritual gift to you so that you can be strengthened. What I mean is that we can mutually encourage each other while I am with you. We can be encouraged by the faithfulness we find in each other, both your faithfulness and mine. (Rom 1:11-12)

Insights from *Just Say Yes!*

Missional Assumption: The Work of the Church Is to Encourage People in Their Callings

"What do we offer the person who is new to the faith and struggling to understand the life and teachings of Christ? Encouragement. The person who is curious about the spiritual life and feeling uncertain about how to pray? Encouragement. The person motivated to offer themselves as a volunteer for the first time? Encouragement. The person who wants to help strangers rebuild their homes or to help the homeless find food and shelter? Encouragement. . . . People discerning their spiritual gifts, wrestling with a call to ministry, searching for God's intention for their lives? Encouragement. The person excited about starting a class or launching a children's ministry? Encouragement. Encouragement means giving someone the strength to change and grow and serve. Real encouragement means helping people say *Yes* to God." (113)

Questions to Ponder

- What is the first thing that comes to mind when you read, "let us consider each other carefully for the purpose of sparking love and good deeds" (Heb 10:24)? Have others sparked love and good deeds in you?

- When is a time you have been encouraged by someone else in your faith? Is there a time when you encouraged someone else in his or her faith?

- The author describes encouragement using phrases and words such as *strength of purpose, give support, give confidence, give hope, inspire, motivate, gently persuade, prod, prompt, embolden, empower, remove restraint, instill resolve, give strength to change, confirm calling* (112–13). Which do you need most to fully use your gifts and answer your calling? Which types of encouragement do you have to offer others?

Prayer

God of steadfast love, thank you for the encouragement we receive through your Holy Spirit. With your power, help us build each other up and mutually encourage faithfulness. Embolden us to spark love and good deeds in others. Inspire us to continually say Yes *to you and motivate us to leave a legacy of encouragement in this world. In the name of Jesus Christ, amen.*

Weekly Challenge

Who were the people you thought of when asked who encourages you in your faith and calling? Take some time to write them a note of encouragement or take them to coffee or tea to encourage them. Prayerfully consider ways you can use your gifts to encourage others to answer their callings in your church. Then just say *Yes* to follow Jesus Christ into the world with courage and hope!